AMERICAN UGLY: Kevin Spacey Beats the Rapp But Dark Secrets Made Public in SDNY LIVE

by Matthew Russell Lee

Inner City Press (c) October 2022

Introduction

Kevin Spaccy on the first day of his defense case dropped a bomb from the Second World War. He said, My father was a neo-Nazi and a white supremacist.

In the courtroom, one of the other journalists muffled a laugh. Judge Kaplan would throw you out of worse if your phone rang or even vibrated too loudly. Laughing at this could be most costly.

Spacey's point seemed to be that he been secretive about his life, including his sexuality, because of his secret Nazi father.

Except it wasn't secret. Kevin Spacey nee Fowler's older brother Randy Fowler had gone public, on a podcast and elsewhere, about their father cutting his hair and mustache like Hitler and sexually abusing him - him meaning Randy, not Kevin.

The cases, then, were about stealing other people's memories and stories. John Barrowman was jumped on by Spacey - Kevin Rapp then had the same story. Barrowman wrote that he drank vodka tonics with Drew Barrymore at the Limelight. But he'd only heard that she was there at the same time, and never saw her.

And Spacey stole Randy's history of rape, then refused to pay to fly him to their mother's death bed to put the matter to bed. It would not rest, but the defense would. And next would come the verdict.

I.

It was the first day of the Anthony Rapp versus Kevin Spacey trial, and damn if it didn't actually start on the first day. By 2 pm the jury was selected and Rapp's lawyer Peter Saghir showed the juror a photo of 14-year-old Anthony, and described him retreating to Spacey's bedroom since all the party attendees were adults. Soon they were gone and Spacey, glassy eyed, was on top of him, grinding against his hip.

Less than an hour later Spacey's attack-dog lawyer Jennifer Keller was telling a different story. Rapp had known that Spacey didn't have an erection, she said, and Rapp knew all about those. She said Rapp was seething with resentment as Spacey's career took off: American Beauty, House of Cards, Rapp couldn't take it. So he repeated again and again that he had been sexually assaulted. But hadn't he willingly done to the Limelight club?

Kurt Wheelock, who had been reporting on the case from the beginning, picking up steam when Spacey appeared as a minor character in the periphery of the Ghislaine Maxwell trial, riding on the Lolita Express, wondered if Keller would take this approach if Rapp were a woman, if this was the more conventional Me Too case. There were other echoes of Ghislaine's trial, Maximum Maxwell, more on Patreon here.

There was the photo of Kevin Spacey with Ghislaine Maxwell, sitting on dual thrones. There was the photo of Spacey on Epstein's plane, with Bill Clinton and Chris Tucker, going to exploit Africa. Spacey seemed to do it tongue in cheek.

But it was still tongue. Where had they gone, and what had they done, on that trip? Kurt Wheelock had dug into it, but with the focus on Epstein, before he was thrown out of the UN which Epstein had funded, and Ghislaine Maxwell spoken at.

Kurt wondered about covering this trial. There was less of an international hook that will Epstein and then Maxwell. It might be more like the Weinstein trial in state court across the street, or even as low as Larry Ray, right here in SDNY. But Ray's victims had been Sarah Lawrence College students, of-age. Rapp had been 14. How many more had there been?

Kurt knew people out in Hollywood, some who had worked with Spacey on his projects. Why had they said nothing? A job was a job.

Among the photographers out on Worth Street were some Kurt knew from the UN. What was the connection of all this to the UN? It was something he would explore.

I. In the Courtroom

OK - Rapp v. Kevin Spacey sex abuse trial opening arguments begin. Kevin Spacey is sitting with two lawyers at the defense table, further from the judge. Rapp is at front table, with three lawyers (whom Inner City Press saw outside the SDNY cafeteria between 1 and 2 pm). Drum roll.

Judge Kaplan: OK, let's bring the jury in... Counsel?

Peter Saghir: We represent Anthony Rapp. To understand this case, you need to know this. When Anthony was just 14 years old, something unacceptable happened. It involved a 26-year-old man, Kevin Spacey

Saghir: You will see Anthony Rapp as a man, but I ask you to remember he was a child. You are going to learn that Mr. Rapp for the majority of his life has had relationships with men, as has Kevin Spacey. But that's irrelevant.

Saghir: Anthony Rapp first performed as an actor in camp in Pennsylvania. He started getting paid work. He had done the musical Evita, and The King and I. His mom supported him in his acting. Anthony is a self-proclaimed nerd...

 Saghir: Acting helped Anthony get out of himself. He was cast in Precious Sons, with Ed Harris. At the same time, Kevin Spacey was in Long Day's Journey Into Night. Anthony and his mom were living on 81st Street near York Avenue. He won an award.

Saghir: At an event, he met Kevin Spacey. Then Anthony's friend John, aged 19, came to visit. They'd done Oliver together. They went together to a matinee of Long Day's Journey into Night. They went backstage to meet the cast, it was a tradition.

 Saghir: Kevin Spacey came down. He invited the two of them out to dinner, then out to the Limelight Club on 6th Avenue and 20th Street, an adult nightclub. Anthony didn't have ID. Spacey talked to the doorman and they got in.

Saghir: Anthony will tell you, music was loud, people were drinking, it wasn't really his scene. Kevin Spacey invites Anthony to a party at his apartment. John will say he was there, and flirting with Kevin Spacey. Anthony came out of the bathroom and John sat up

Saghir: For the party, another night, Anthony walked south to the 60s. The apartment has a view of NYC. It's a gathering of 5 or 6 people. Anthony only recognizes Kevin Spacey. They are all adults. So he goes into the bedroom to watch TV.

Saghir: Kevin Spacey comes into the bedroom. He is unsteady on his feet. He is intoxicated. The people from the party had left. He's alone with Kevin Spacey in his bedroom. No words were spoken. Kevin Spacey puts his hand under Anthony's butt

Saghir: Kevin Spacey picks Anthony up like a groom would. Spacey lays Anthony down on the bed. Anthony is 5'5", 100 pounds. Kevin Spacey climbs on top of him, and grinds his pelvis against the side of his hip. Anthony is shocked.

Saghir: Anthony's hands are smushed to the side. This was not horseplay. We will prove that Kevin Spacey did his to gratify his own sexual desires. Anthony wriggles out and escapes to the bathroom. He runs out to the front door. Kevin Spacey follows him.

Saghir: Kevin Spacey says, Are you sure you want to go? Kevin Spacey is trying to get him to stay, to gratify his sexual desires. Back in Illinois, Anthony tells a friend what Kevin Spacey did... Time went up, Spacey became better known

Saghir: Anthony's friends ask him, Did you see "L.A. Confidential?" And he remembers what happened in that bedroom. This violation at the age of 14 has impacted Anthony, he will describe how. It was no mistake. This was a deliberate act.

Saghir: You will hear in this trial from another man... Anthony read an article, about the author's encounter with Harvey Weinstein. He feels it was similar. And feels, maybe he can hold Kevin Spacey to account. He speaks to a reporter, and a story is published

Saghir: Kevin Spacey responded to the article with a statement on Twitter: I have a lot of respect for Anthony Rapp as an actor... I do not remember the encounter. If I did it, I owe him an apology... I now live as a gay man. But not a word about the 14-year-old.

 Saghir: Afterward, Kevin Spacey says his memory changed, it never happened, Anthony is a liar. Both sides took depositions; we deposed Spacey. After that tweet, he went through boxes and boxes of documents. Now he claims it was a studio apartment.

Saghir: He wrote a draft before the tweet, he wrote that he took drugs & drank a lot. When asked he said he meant 1987, not 1986. He's retreating from his words. We retained Lisa Roccio. She found no malingering & no exaggeration. But Spacey retained Dr Loftus...

Saghir: We will ask you, jurors, to render a verdict of 100% justice. Thank you for your time.

 Judge Kaplan: Defense?

Jennifer Keller: My client Kevin Spacey wants justice. This case is about whether you think this happened. It is not a trial of every other rumor

Keller: It's not about if you like Frank Underwood. It's about this thing - did it happen? Mr. Rapp is now 50. He created a story and it grew. He has been repeating this same false story. Never went to the police. He'd say it when he saw Kevin Space get an Oscar

Keller: He's been telling this story to raise his own profile. He never became the international star Kevin Spacey did. He has been simmering with resentment. It's not easy to defend this, after 30 years.

Keller: Anthony's mother gave up her career as a nurse to help Anthony. But Anthony wanted to spread his wings. He wrote a book about this, about his life. He'd hit his mother in the face, knocked her glasses off.

 Keller: Yes Kevin Spacey had to go through boxes and boxes to find out which apartment he was living in then. He is a packrat. But he found the lease. It was one room. You could see everything.

Keller: Because Anthony Rapp never went to the police, it never got checked out. He can't say who the guests were. Facts are stubborn things. And John, when he was deposed, told the story about the Limelight, then that they went to the apartment.

Keller: The reality is that Mr. Spacey was interested in John, not Anthony. Mr. Spacey called John and his mother in Illinois. They both have ancestors from Scotland. This story does not match up with the facts, or this other witness. It just doesn't.

Keller: Why make up a bedroom story? Well, being surprised that all the guests had left only make sense if there is a separate room. Let's see what Mr. Rapp said. [Plays deposition, questions about windows and doors]

 Keller: Mr. Rapp did not detect any erection, and he knew what that was. Mr. Rapp described Mr. Spacey as having been a dead weight.

 Keller: As Mr. Spacey's star rose, Mr. Rapp grew resentful. "Rent" was the apex of his career. He peaked in 2000 and grew bitter. So he became an out gay actor. I don't know if he would have been a leading man anyway.

Keller: Mr. Rapp knew that Mr. Spacey was in the closet, and through he could be doing things for the gay community. Mr. Rapp would go to Oscar parties and tell people about what Mr. Spacey supposedly done to him. He threw pencils at the screen one year.

 Keller: It's not a true story, but he did tell it a lot. Mr. Rapp blames everything on Mr. Spacey - that he cheated on his boyfriend, and that he cannot assert himself in sexual relationship. We'll show you different. He forgets his lines? It's Mr. Spacey.

 Keller: He doesn't want to seem to want to talk about other traumas. He claims Yul Brenner punched him at 10 years old, he says. But he doesn't want to talk about it. Please use your common sense when you listen to Dr. Roccio. There was no PTSD.

 Keller: What about this tweet that Mr. Spacey sent? It was right after the Harvey Weinstein allegations. All sorts of people are worried about being canceled. Here comes Mr. Rapp. It is panic, among Mr. Spacey's business manager and agent

Keller: This is one of the cardinal rules of the so-called #MeToo movement, that you have to believe the victim. You'll see that Mr. Spacey said, this didn't happen, I don't remember it. They told him to apologize. It was cleverly set up by Mr. Rapp

Keller: Mr. Rapp didn't go to the New York Times. He didn't even go to the New York Post... This so-called independent journalist was a personal friend of Mr. Rapp. They plotted together to nail Mr. Spacey.

Keller: Mr. Spacey was only trying to be respectful to Mr. Rapp, he was asking, Could it have happened? They made him apologize to keep the social media mob from coming after him. Mr. Spacey knew he had never been attracted to kids.

Keller: This book Rapp wrote, it was supposedly about "Rent" - but it was about him. And it didn't have this story on it, even anonymized... Mr. Rapp had a lot of therapy. He had one therapist for twenty years - twenty years. Never mentioned Mr. Spacey.

Keller: I know it is a super-charged environment we live in these days. But you all are not super-charged. There is no liability here. Thank you. Judge Kaplan: OK folks, that's it for the day.

II.

Another victim of Kevin Spacey was the first witness called by Anthony Rapp. His name was Andrew Holtzman and he had been working for Joe Papp in the Public Theater in Astor Place, in a secluded office that other people sometimes came in to share, when Spacey jumped him.

Holtzman said he looked up and Spacey took his windbreaker off, showing off tight jeans and what was inside them. Then Spacey picked up him and thrust himself against him.

On cross examination, Spacey's lawyer Scolnick made a joke of it, asking Why he jump over the desk in a single bound?

Rapp's lawyer objected, but it may have been too late, Kurt Wheelock thought. After a friend of Rapp's, Chris Denny, who said he'd heard the Kevin Spacey story, Anthony himself took the stand. As he tried to tell the jurors about his initially meteoric acting career, Scolnick repeatedly cut in and objected, saying "Irrelevant."

And the judge agreed, sustaining the objection again and again. By day's end, he asked

Spacey's lawyer is he would be making a motion under Rule 50, for a directed verdict. Yes, Team Spacey said, they would so move on all counts.

II. In the Courtroom

Jury entering! First witness is Andrew Holtzman [yet another Holtzman accuser. He married his husband in 2009.]

Rapp's lawyer: Let me direct your attention to 1991. Where were you working?

Holtzman: Joseph Papp's NY Shakespeare Festival on Lafayette Street.

Rapp's lawyer: Tell us who Joseph Papp is.

Judge Kaplan: Sustained. Get to the point.

Rapp's lawyer: Did you work in a full program there?

Holtzman: Yes. For Mr. Papp's wife. I told to know Mr. Papp when he came in. I came to run a second-change film office

 Rapp's lawyer: Describe the office. Holtzman:

There were two desks. Rapp's lawyer: Did you encounter Kevin Spacey?

Holtzman: Yes, in the office. I was finishing up a phone call. He was wearing tight blue jeans. I saw that he was erect - then on top of me

Holtzman: He grabbed me by the crotch - for leverage - & I felt his erection against my body. He had not said anything. I was shouting. After a time he pulled away & looked angry, like it wasn't supposed to go this way

Spacey's lawyer: Objection.

Judge: Sustained.

Judge Kaplan: Everything after angry is stricken. Rapp's lawyer: What did you think?

Spacey's lawyer: Objection.

Judge: Sustained.

Rapp's lawyer: What did you do next? Holtzman: I sat at my desk. [Judge Kaplan calls lawyer for a whispered sidebar]

Judge Kaplan: Cross examination.

Spacey's lawyer: You understand we're here about a party in 1986, right?

Holtzman: Yes.

Spacey's lawyer: You have no first-hand knowledge of that party, correct?

Holtzman: No first-hand knowledge.

 Spacey's lawyer: In 1991 you were 27, right?

Holtzman: Yes. Spacey's lawyer: You had chest hair?

Holtzman: Some.

Spacey's lawyer: You felt comfortable with Mr. Papp, and were open with him about your sexual orientation, yes?

Holtzman: Yes.

Spacey's lawyer Scolnick: Mr. Papp gave your outrageous opportunities, right?

Holtzman: If I said that. Scolnick: You can't explain how you knew it was Kevin Spacey when he came into the office, right?

Holtzman: I can--

Scolnick: Yes or no.

Scolnick: Other people came in to use the 2d desk, yes? Holtzman: At certain times of the year. Scolnick: Your deposition, you could review it, yes? Judge Kaplan: Let's save time. Just read from the transcript, then ask the witness about it.

Holtzman: He lifted me up on the desk. Judge Kaplan: How much did you weight then?

Holtzman: 120 or 130. Judge: Thanks. Scolnick: Did he leap over your desk in a single bound? Rapp's lawyer: Objection. Judge Kaplan: Sustained, argumentative, Superman.

Scolnick: You screamed but no one came in, right? Holtzman: We haven't discussed where the office was. Scolnick: You didn't see him again, correct? Holtzman: Yes, thankfully. I wasn't looking for him.

Scolnick: Isn't it true you were present at the film screenings, along with Mr. Fabiano Espinoso, yes?

Holtzman: I'm not arguing he wasn't.

Scolnick: Now there's a Joe's Pub, right?

Holtzman: There wasn't then.

 Scolnick: That was the entrance, and Mr. Spacey sat there with Dolores, right?

Holtzman: I never saw him. I'm being truthful, I'm under oath. Dolores was a wonderful character. I never saw Kevin Spacey again.

Scolnick: Mr. Spacey was an assistant to Mr. Papp, yes?

Holtzman: Not that I remember. I can name two other names.

Scolnick: You never told Mr. Papp about your Kevin Spacey story, right?

Holtzman: I didn't tell anyone at the Public Theater.

Scolnick: You told it for the first time on Facebook in 2017, yes?

Holtzman: To my friends.

Scolnick: And there were 58 responses, by people who did not know the story, right?

Holtzman: They were very compassionate.

Scolnick: You kept a journal, didn't you?
Holtzman: I couldn't find them.

Scolnick: I asked you for a copy of these alleged journals, right?

Holtzman: We keep a lot of things over the years, and some don't last.

Scolnick: Mr. Papp could have ended Mr. Spacey's career, yes?

Holtzman: I suppose.

Scolnick: Nothing further.

Judge: Re-direct.

Rapp's lawyer: You said you didn't want to see the play Henry IV. Why not?

Scolnick: Objection!

Judge: Sustained.

Rapp's lawyer: You said retribution, meaning what? Holtzman: I was frightened and confused, I thought Kevin Spacey might tell Mr. Papp I'd done something.

Rapp's lawyer: Who were the secretaries to Mr. Papp?

Holtzman: Louise, the guardian to Mr. Trump, I mean Papp

Rapp's lawyer: Had you told people about what Spacey did?

 Holtzman: Yes. We'd be watching the Oscars and people would bring him up. And if comfortable I'd tell the story.

Rapp's lawyer: Any doubt it was Mr. Spacey?

Holtzman: None.

Rapp's lawyer: Nothing further.

After a break, next witness is Christopher Denny. He came NYC in 1979 with "stars in his eyes for music and theater. His mother was on Broadway in the 50s.

Rapp's lawyer: How did you meet Anthony Rapp?

Denny: He was in an off-Broadway play called Sophistry.

Rapp's lawyer: Did Anthony tell you what happened with Mr. Spacey?

Denny: Yes. He told me he went to a side room to watch TV. That Spacey came in and got on top of him...

Cross examination.

Spacey's lawyer: Let me know you your deposition testimony.

Denny: Let me get my glasses out (sighs).

Spacey's lawyer (reading) you said, a door or something.

Denny: May I explain? Judge: This is not an essay question.

Spacey's lawyer: Did you read Mr. Rapp's book, the part about abusing his partner?

Denny: Somewhat.

Judge: Next witness.

Rapp's lawyer: Next is a video deposition of Sean Snow, who says "picked up like a bride"

Q: How did you meet Mr. Rapp?

Snow: On the set of School Ties, in 1991. Then I moved to NYC in 1992.

Q: Did he ever have an unhealthy relationship?

Snow: Yes, with Joshua Safron, who is deeply insecure. He was parsimonious in his praise of Anthony

Q: Have you ever had a romantic relationship with Mr. Rapp?

Snow: No. End of video.

Next witness... Anthony Rapp. Drum roll.

There was an hour-long lunch break. Here's Rapp. Rapp's lawyer: Anthony, where do you live?

Rapp: The East Village. With my husband Ken.

Rapp's lawyer: Where did you go to college?

Rapp: To NYU for a short time. They didn't have any financial aid left for me.

Rapp's lawyer: Tell me about the plays you were in.

Judge Kaplan: Can we move this along to something more relevant?

Rapp's lawyer: May we have a sidebar?

Judge: No.

Rapp's lawyer: Tell me about one play. Rapp: At 9 I was an understudy to Tiny Tim.

 Rapp: I was looking for work, I got a job at Starbucks - then I got the part in Rent. I was in it for 2 years.

Rapp's lawyer: What awards did Rent win?

Rapp: The Tony, and the Pulitzer Prize posthumously.

Rapp's lawyer: How about TV?

Rapp: I did Law & Order SVU. I was on Star Trek Discovery. We're filming our fifth season now. My character is openly gay.

Rapp's lawyer: What was it like, to be cast as the first openly gay character in Star Trek?

Spacey's lawyer: Objection, irrelevant.

Judge Kaplan: Sustained.

Rapp's lawyer: Who was a mentor to you?

 Rapp: Ed Harris.

Rapp's lawyer: How do you choose your projects?

Spacey's lawyer: Objection, irrelevant.

Judge Kaplan: Sustained.

Rapp's lawyer: Can we have a sidebar?

Judge: No.

Rapp's lawyer: Let's talk about your sexual orientation.

Rapp: Larry Kramer was a-

Spacey's lawyer: Objection, non-responsive and irrelevant.

Judge Kaplan: It is stricken.

Rapp's lawyer: How was working with adults?

Rapp: Yul Brenner told me, "Get out of my way!"

Rapp's lawyer: You can to NYC to do Precious Sons?

Rapp: Yes. Ed Harris played my father. It was a great time. I was going to Tower Records, I was in the theater community.

Rapp's lawyer: You met Kevin Spacey?

Rapp: At a function. I knew that he was in Long Day's Journey into Night.

Rapp: I also met Lilly Tomlin... I felt I was treated like a peer.

Rapp's lawyer: When you went backstage at Long Day's Journey into Night, what happened?

Rapp: There's a private area. Kevin Spacey received us.

Rapp: I congratulated him as I had Jack Lemmon, who'd met us first. Later we went out to dinner with Kevin Spacey.

Rapp's lawyer: Then where did you go?

Rapp: The Limelight nightclub. I'd never been there and I had no ID. Kevin Spacey got me in.

 Rapp: Later he had a party on the Upper East Side. I walked from 81st to off of 2nd Ave in the 60s, a tall black glass high rise. Upstairs, Kevin Spacey was the only one I knew. I went to the window, and I saw the bedroom with the TV in it, to the side.

Rapp's lawyer: Did you draw the apartment at your deposition?

Rapp: I did...

Rapp's lawyer: In the incident, where was his torso?

Rapp: On mine. But not parallel.

Rapp's lawyer: What were you thinking?

Rapp: I was (pause) I knew something was really wrong

Rapp's lawyer: What did you think when he said Are you sure you want to leave?

Spacey's lawyer: Objection, calls for speculation.

Judge Kaplan: Overruled.

Rapp: That he wanted me to stay. But I left.

Judge Kaplan: I promised the jurors they could leave at 3:30, so they can. Mr. Rapp, step down. Counsel, please remain.

And then Judge Kaplan asks the defense, Will you be making a Rule 50 motion? Yes.

Judge Kaplan: I'm not forecasting my ruling...

III.

There were, it turned out, supporters of Kevin Spacey, in a way there had not been for Ghislaine Maxwell. It was that he was an actor; some people who liked his movies felt they knew him, that he couldn't have done this or if it had it didn't matter.

Kurt who had tried to live tweet Day 1 without commentary found himself accused of being "too tabloid" - even as he cut out words like "erection" which Andrew Holtzman had used. Nor did he want to make Judge Kaplan look as opinionated as he was coming off.

Down on Worth Street, two photographers he'd know at the UN greeted him. This time Kurt got some video of Spacey, of him not answering Kurt's shouted question about Judge Kaplan denying Rapp's request for sidebars. Spacey drove or was driven away in a big SUV with tinted windows. He might soon be taking a victory lap.

IV.

Now Anthony Rapp was on the stand, or on the cross, under cross examination by Kevin Spacey's lawyer. She mocked him, as selling only 26 CDs of his music. She repeatedly implied that the basis for his accusation was that he was jealous of Spacey and his movies, which she mentioned in turn.

You threw pencils at the TV screen when Kevin Spacey won the Oscar, didn't you, she asked.

One pencil, Rapp insisted.

American Beauty was very well received, wasn't it, she asked.

He supposed it was, adding how the predator - or was it slacker? - character Spacey played, Lester Burnham, made him feel. This became a worldwide lead. The coverage was defendant-centric. This was true in the Ghislaine Maxwell trial too, Kurt Wheelock supposed. But this was different. While live tweeting that trial, he had got over the transom almost no defense of Ghislaine. Here he was hearing from Spacey supporters, and perhaps separately, from MeToo doubters.

Rapp had said he decided to go public once he read an op-ed about Harvey Weinstein. But it turned out that was published five days later. Did that mean Kevin Spacey was not a predator? Kurt Wheelock thought, and sang, No. But would the jury doubt Rapp?

IV. In the Courtroom

OK - in Kevin Spacey trial, Anthony Rapp is still on the stand on direct examination.

Rapp's lawyer: I want to direct your attention back to Precious Sons, and how Ed Harris held you in that play. Was it similar to how Kevin Spacey picked you up, like a bride?

Rapp: With Ed Harris, it was loving, nothing sexual about it.

Rapp's lawyer: When if ever did Ed Harris grind his pelvis into you? Rapp: Never.

Rapp's lawyer: When if ever did you feel Ed Harris was trying to get with you sexually?

Spacey's lawyer: Objection! Relevance.

Judge: Sustained. Rapp's lawyer: Where did you go next? Rapp: Interlochen, the rigorous music camp.

Rapp's lawyer: When did it come back to you? Rapp: I went to see "Working Girl" in my local cinema, and saw him on the screen and it was like someone poked me with a cattle prod.

Rapp's lawyer: Have you watched others of his films? Rapp: Usual Suspects, LA Confidential, American Beauty...

Rapp's lawyer: Why did you go to them? Rapp: I am an actor. I felt it was part of my job to go see them. I steeled myself and tamped it down

Rapp's lawyer: Have you seen Kevin Spacey in a play? Rapp: Yes, Lost in Yonkers. Rapp's lawyer: And television?

Rapp: Only on award shows. Rapp's lawyer: Did you attend Oscar parties? Rapp: Yes, at Elizabeth Law's on the Upper East Side.

Rapp's lawyer: What about you throwing pencils at the screen, as was brought up earlier in the trial?

Rapp: Elizabeth use to throw a rubber chicken at

the screen. I threw a pencil, my version. I had watched the Oscars since I was a kid.

 Rapp: I was at an event, in a large bathroom, and Kevin Spacey walked in. It was startling to be in his gaze. I wanted to get out. I went out.

Rapp's lawyer: Anthony, have you ever written a tell-all book?

Rapp: Not a tell-all. A memoir of love, focused only on the time I was in Rent, the workshop production, the off-Broadway, my mother - a three-year period is the main thrust

 Rapp's lawyer: When did you mother give up her career for yours?

Rapp: She only put it on pause until she went back to Joliet... Once when I was 13, she slapped me. I said, I will slap you back. Then the next year in NY, she came in and slapped me. I slapped back

Rapp's lawyer: Did you fight with a boyfriend?
Rapp: Yes, Josh Safron. We were in an alleyway by the theater, a Sunday in July. He said, Never talk to me again. I saw red and I launched myself at

him and knocked him down.

 Rapp's lawyer: What did you do after that fight?

Spacey's lawyer: Objection to the characterization as a fight.

 Judge: Sustained. Rapp's lawyer: After the altercation -- Spacey's lawyer: Objection. Judge: Sustained.

 Rapp's lawyer: When you get the interviews about these events, what concerns did you have? Rapp: I had already told my producers and the PR people of Star Trek Discovery I was contemplating doing this. I was aware Kevin Spacey was in the middle of House of Cards

Rapp's lawyer: Did you want a career like Kevin Spacey's? Rapp: No, I was fine with what I had. I could be picky about projects... I read about Me Too & Harvey Weinstein, I identified with it

Rapp's lawyer: How has the case been? Rapp: I was in line to enter the building this morning and Kevin Spacey was there. It was hard to breathe.

Rapp's lawyer: When if ever have you regretted bringing this lawsuit? Spacey's lawyer: Objection Judge: Sustained

Rapp: I brought this lawsuit hoping I could help protect others. Judge Kaplan: Strike that last remark. [Rapp drinks from bottle of water, closes his eyes]

Rapp's lawyer: No further questions. Judge: We'll take a break.

Jury entering! Judge Kaplan: Cross-examination. Ms. Keller. Spacey's lawyer Keller: This is the article where you went public, right? Rapp: Yes.

Keller: You decided in a quiet moment by the window, yes? Rapp: What do you mean? Keller: You said that.

Keller: Lupita Nyong'o is a legitimate star, right? Rapp: Yes.

Keller: She had a meteoric rise, correct? Rapp: Yes. Keller: Let's look at your deposition. You said you were moved. True? Rapp: I was.

Rapp's lawyer: Can she read the whole question? Judge Kaplan: I'll read it... No, move on. Keller: You got an award for accusing Mr. Spacey, yes? Rapp's lawyer: Objection, relevance. Keller: I can make an offer of proof. Judge Kaplan: Not necessary. Overruled.

Keller: You wrote to Vary of Buzzfeed that you wanted to expose someone powerful but do it in the best way, right?

Rapp: Can I see that? Keller: Yes. And this was before the op-ed by Ms. Nyong'o - five days before, Vary told you Buzzfeed wanted you to have impact

Keller: So in the article, you claim Mr. Spacey picked you and Mr. Barrowman out and invited you to the Limelight clubs, right? Rapp's lawyer: Objection - misstates the evidence. Judge Kaplan: Overruled.

Keller: You didn't tell Mr. Vary one word about Jack Lemmon that night, did you? Rapp: I don't know that for certain. Keller: Do you think night clubs in NYC are fully going at 8 pm?

Rapp: I had no way to know at the time. Keller:

How old are you now? Rapp: 50. Keller: And you don't know when things start? Rapp: I haven't been to a club in a while.

Keller: You told Vary that it was fun at the Limelight, yes?

Rapp: I did. The conversation was good, but at the club, I couldn't hear. Keller: So it was fun, or it was unpleasant - which one?

Keller: Mr. Spacey was flirting with Mr. Barrowman, right? Rapp: I don't recall. Keller: You claim only you were invited to the party at Mr. Spacey's apartment, yes? Rapp: That's my recollection.

Keller: You say you made your way safely home - was danger lurking? Rapp: I wouldn't say that. Keller: But you did, in your deposition on page 37, lines 18 to 24.

 Keller: Mr. Barrowman says Mr. Spacey had a dog, a brown lab - and you've never mentioned it, right? Rapp: I do not remember a brown dog.

 Judge Kaplan: Ms., Keller, how much more do you

have? Keller: Quite a bit. Judge: Jurors may take a break. Thread will continue.

OK - they're back. Keller: Let's talk more about Mr. Barrowman. You went radio silence with him?

Rapp: We weren't close friends. Judge: Answer the question. You know what radio silence is. Rapp: It sounds intentional. Judge: I'm not going to quibble with you

Keller: In your book, you say you were growing restless with your mother's presence, right? Rapp: Only during rehearsals.

Keller: Come on, wasn't it because your brother was molested by her boyfriend? Rapp: I wasn't aware of that then. Keller: You say that at Mr. Spacey's, when you went into be bedroom, David Letterman was on TV, right?

Rapp: Yes. Keller: And he had the Late Night Show? Rapp: I don't know what it was called.

Keller: The first time you were really questioned about your Kevin Spacey story was in your deposition in this case, right? Rapp: No. Vary questioned me. Keller: Your good friend, who said he would leave things vague so Mr. Spenser could not rebut - that friend?

Keller: So when Mr. Spacey's body was on you, he didn't touch your p*nis, did he?

Rapp: No. Keller: He didn't try to get you to touch his, did he? Rapp: He did not. Keller: How long was he on top? Rapp: It was a frozen moment for me. Keller: That's not my question

Keller: And when you tried to leave, you're saying Mr. Spacey was at the door, right? Rapp: Yes. Keller: But you don't know how he got there... I know you're on Star Trek Discovery, but you're not alleging he used a transporter, are you? Break taken.

They're back. Keller: Buzzfeed reported that you wanted to shout, This guy is a fraud, right? Rapp: Is that in the article? Keller: Yes. You thought he was portraying himself as straight, correct? Rapp: Yes.

Keller: You called yourself queer? Rapp: Yes.

Keller: Did you end a relationship with a boyfriend

because he wouldn't come out as gay?

 Rapp: May I explain? It was because he would not be photographed with me at an event for the play "Rent" Keller: Because that would out him, right? Rapp: Yes.

 Keller: Kevin Spacey's star rose, and you were having trouble getting media attention, true? Rapp: When are you referring to?

Keller: 1996 and onward. Rapp: That is not accurate. Keller: Kevin Spacey was in L.A. Confidential, and you went to see him in it? Rapp: Yes

Keller: When you put out a CD and went to sell it on a college campus, you sold only 26 CDs, right?

Rapp: Did I say "only"? Judge Kaplan: Are you saying that selling 26 CDs after a concert is a success? Rapp: At that concert, yes.

Keller: You were in "You're a Good Man, Charlie Brown." You couldn't claim that's in the same league at The Iceman Cometh, right? Rapp: They are different kinds of shows.

Judge Kaplan: We'll break here.

V.

Jennifer Keller got into the black SUV with Kevin Spacey when the trial day was done. There were shouted questions - Kurt Wheelock asked if Spacey thought of the judge's rulings - but no answers.

Anthony Rapp had been put through the ringer, not only by Keller but also the judge. Several times he closed his eyes, and not for short periods of time. At one point Kurt prepared a tweet that Rapp's hands were shaking, as he drank from a bottle of water. Then he deleted it. The dialogue said more than enough.

At the beginning of the trial, now only three days in, those who seemed to be or openly identified as Spacey supporters and/or doubters of McToo thanked Kurt for his "objective" feed.

Then when over the Columbus Day break Kurt wrote and uploaded a short rhyming song, with a refrain that "Kevin Spacey is a predator, An X-rated version of Roger Federer," he got push back.

Understandably from Roger Federer supporters (while the use of private jets was the connection, if Kurt redid the song he'd rhyme predator with creditor, or Redditor), but more vehemently from Spacey supporters. It was true Kurt didn't sing (or write rhymes to be sung) in the way he tweeted.

He thought, maybe the line should have been, Kevin Spacey PLAYS a predator - that would link back into what others had chosen as the lead of Day 3, that Rapp was sickened by the predatory Lester Burnham character Spacey had played in American Beauty.

Keller, seemingly gratuitously, brought out that Rapp's mother's boyfriend had molested his brother. Was this the way victims were dissuaded, that not only them but their families would be dragged through the mud? But that was Spacey's line, that he was being dragged through the mud. It was civil litigation, down and dirty. Kurt would follow it to the end.

VI.

Plaintiff Anthony Rapp had been crossed and re-crossed, had been asked about hitting his mother and being hit by his now husband when at least the "next witness" was called.

He was Chris Hart, Rapp's friend from Joliet, now flown in from San Francisco on the dime of Rapp's law firm and staying overnight at the Hampton Inn. But that wasn't what Kevin Spacey's lawyers wanted to know. A question was asked on cross; Rule 412 was invoked and soon Judge Kaplan was ordering everyone including Kurt Wheelock out of the courtroom.

Kurt went down to the SDNY Magistrates Court and covered a few cases; he went up to Judge Woods' on the 12 floor and sat with the
Marshals waiting to handcuff and remand a defendant who'd just pled guilty to being a felon in possession of a firearm.

But when Wheelock went back up to 21, the courtroom was still sealed. He went back down to his laptop in the Press Room and looked up Rule 412:

Rule 412. Sex-Offense Cases: The Victim Primary tabs (a) Prohibited Uses. The following evidence is not admissible in a civil or criminal proceeding involving alleged sexual misconduct: (1) evidence offered to prove that a victim engaged in other sexual behavior; or (2) evidence offered to prove a victim's sexual predisposition. (b) Exceptions. (1) Criminal Cases. The court may admit the following evidence in a criminal case: (A) evidence of specific instances of a victim's sexual behavior, if offered to prove that someone other than the defendant was the source of semen, injury, or other physical evidence... Hearing. Before admitting evidence under this rule, the court must conduct an in camera hearing and give the victim and parties a right to attend and be heard. Unless the court orders otherwise, the motion, related materials, and the record of the hearing must be and remain sealed. (d) Definition of "Victim." In this rule, "victim" includes an alleged victim.

But had the rule really been written for this? Kurt finally got back in as $450 dollar an hour expert

Rocchio took the stand, as she had in the Ghislaine Maxwell trial.

VI. In the Courtroom - then out of it

On October 12, Day 4, Rapp was cross examined to the end - then under Rule 412, a courtroom closure. Thread here:

OK - Kevin Spacey trial has just resumed, with Anthony Rapp under cross examination by Spacey's lawyer Jennifer Keller. Before jury enters, Judge Kaplan says Keller should asked Rapp, Did you say in substance, and that Rapp (who he calls a smart young man - at 50 - has the job of answering questions. It begins.

Keller: You were comfortable with your therapist, yes? Rapp: Yes. Keller: You are claiming that the incident that you say happened with Mr. Spacey has permeated relationships throughout your life, correct?

Rapp: Yes. Keller: But you didn't tell your doctor your Kevin Spacey story, did you? Rapp: I did not.

Keller: You told dozens of people your Kevin Spacey story before ever telling your therapist of many decades, true? Rapp: Yes. Keller: You told her upsetting details about your private life, right? About attacking your boyfriend, yes? Rapp: Yes.

Keller: You told her about other attacks on you, including being physically attacked, right? Rapp: I may have. Keller: Your book Without You anonymized some of your sexual partners, right? Rapp: Yes. Keller: But not an anonymous actor jumping on you? Rapp: No.

Keller: Isn't Buzzfeed known for quizzes about celebrities and food?

Rapp: There's also News. Keller: And didn't Mr. Vary tell you, We can't place Mr. Spacey at the Tony's? "We'll say you saw him at an industry event." Rapp: That's what he said.

Keller: Is that a reporter of integrity? Rapp: To some degree. May I explain? Judge: Your lawyer will have an opportunity. Answer these questions.

Keller: You complained to Mr. Vary that you weren't nominated, and he was outraged for you? Rapp: I don't recall this

Keller: Your profile has been raised by making these claims, right?

Rapp: I don't know how to measure that. Keller: Well, Adam Rapp was not a household name, and probably still isn't. Rapp: Adam Rapp is my brother. Keller: I haven't had my 3d cup of coffee yet

Keller: You accused Yul Brenner of hitting you in the stomach - and made the accusation after he died, right? Rapp: I do not remember this article. Keller: Does this Refresh your memory? Rapp: No. Keller: You said, He punched me and said Get out of my way.

Keller: And did you tell your Yul Brenner story every time he was up for an award? Moving this article as an exhibit. Judge Kaplan: You should have these ready, with a copy for me. I've been doing this for 28 years. Keller: May I have a moment? Judge: Yes.

Keller: Haven't you said that your husband abused you? Rapp: Once he pushed me down and I fell on my butt.

Keller: And another time he slapped you and hit you in the shoulder, yes? Rapp: I believe so. Judge: Did you say that? Rapp: In substance, yes.

Keller: You are claiming that this incident impacted your approach to sex, yes? Rapp: Yes. Keller: Aren't pubescent males generally aware of sex? (Laughs) C'mon, Mr. Rapp. Rapp's lawyer:

Objection. Judge: Overruled. You listen carefully as it's read back.

Now re-direct. Rapp's lawyer: What was the relationship between the Harvey Weinstein op-ed and what you told Vary? Rapp: I was at the early stage, I still had to talk with Ken and my producers. Then I saw the piece and I decided to move forward.

Rapp's lawyer: What did Mr. Barrowman say? Rapp: That Spacey was touching his leg under the table all night. He said it was unwanted. Rapp's lawyer: Why don't you remember who else was at Spacey's party? Rapp: Because it's the bedroom that's seared on my memory

Rapp's lawyer: You were asked about American Beauty, what was difficult? Rapp: Seeing him in the film pursuing sexual relations with a teenage girl. Judge Kaplan calls a break, asks how much more re-direct. 10 minutes, apparently. Thread will continue.

Rapp's lawyer: Anthony, why did you come forward? Rapp: Because I know that Kevin Spacey has abused others, too. Judge Kaplan: Strike that answer. Rapp's lawyer: May we be heard? [Whispered sidebar ensues; Rapp is still on the stand]

Now re-cross. Keller: You said Kevin Spacey's character in American Beauty has sex with a teenage girl. But he doesn't, right? Rapp: I don't recall that. Keller: Judge Kaplan said, Don't try this case in the media, right? Rapp's lawyer: Objection... No, withdrawn

Judge Kaplan: Tell me we're not going to have the movie shown... I mean it, I want a stipulation. Q: To the facts of the movie? Judge Kaplan: Yes. Next witness: Christopher Hart.

Rapp's lawyer: What did you say, when Anthony Rapp told you what Kevin Spacey had done to him? Hart: I don't remember what I said, but I do remember him telling me. Rapp's lawyer: Did Anthony ever say he had a crush on John Barrowman? Hart: Never.

Rapp's lawyer: Who paid for your flight here from SF? Hart: Your firm. Cross examination. Spacey's lawyer Scolnick: You have no first-hand knowledge if Mr. Rapp's claims are true, right?

Hart: No first-hand knowledge.

Scolnick: Anthony Rapp didn't tell you he went to Jack Lemmon's dressing room, did he? Hart: He did not. Scolnick: Did he tell you Ed Harris' character pretended to make a sexual advance on him in every performance? Hart: No.

An objection is made "under Rule 412." Judge Kaplan tells not only the jurors, but also the spectators (and press) to leave the courtroom.

VII.

Kurt Wheelock's way was to ask to unseal everything. But here the idea was that the sealing of the courtroom was to protect the victim, or victims. Was it so Chris Hart couldn't be asked of or if sex with Rapp? It was ostensibly being inquired into to show bias of the witness, not to blame Rapp for what he had done or not done at age 14.

When finally, back in the courtroom, Kurt had lost his seat, and so took one on the bench in the back. He had a better view for the jury, not undiverse. So too those in the gallery. Usually these SDNY courtroom galleries were empty, or for sentencings sometimes had family members, a baby crying out.

For a still ongoing criminal crypto case, a Haitian entrepreneur filled the pews with his supporters or victims, the Court Security Officers kept asking Kurt which he thought they were. They asked about Spacey too, whether the claim was too old, how it could still be brought - and, today, how it was that the courtroom had been cleared.

Rocchio in the front said she was getting $450 an hour, and had been deposed for an entire day by Spacey's lawyers. In the Trevor Milton trial, now paused more than a week by a stated positive COVID test for Milton's lawyer Marc Mukasey, the Harvard securities professor expert was pulling in $1250 an hour, plus a cut from the consultant he brought on. Sex experts made more than the CJA criminal lawyers, but less than the pro-Wall Street Harvard professors. This was American Ugly.

VIII.

For days, Kevin Spacey's lawyer Jennifer Keller had been hammering away at plaintiff Kevin Rapp, implying then outright saying that his allegation for sexual assault was all based on envy for Spacey's career.

Now on October 13 it was announced she'd tested positive for COVID. Kurt Wheelock had seen her, just the day before, piling into the black SUV with Spacey. Judge Kaplan started talking as if the trial would be suspended at least until next Wednesday, with jurors having to test themselves on Sunday and again on Tuesday.

But then no. Judge Kaplan announced that the trial would proceed, with Rapp's expert Rocchio on the stand and now the cross examination not done by Keller. Her fill in was just as vicious, eliciting from Rocchio that Rapp had engaged in oral sex at 11, before the encounter or incident with Kevin Spacey.

XIII. In the Courtroom

OK - or not. Kevin Spacey trial hits problem - his lawyer Jennifer Keller has tested positive for COVID. Judge Kaplan: We must tell the jury.

Judge Kaplan: It may be she is not permitted to enter the courthouse for ten days. So... I propose we call the jurors in and tell them, we're suspended. They'll have to get tested on Sunday and Tuesday

Judge Kaplan: If they're all full vaccinated... Lawyer: But you asked them. Judge Kaplan: Not if they were full vaccinated. If they are full vaccinated and don't have ongoing exposure... We can send them home and tell them we'll advise them

Judge Kaplan: I'd like the defense table and anyone else whose been within six feet of Ms. Keller for more than 10 minutes to stand up - and then put on a mask. If we don't have enough, we'll get more.

Jury entering! Judge Kaplan: Good morning. Ms. Keller has tested positive for the virus. Under the protocol that the Court is following, you folks must test on Sunday and Tuesday, PCR or FDA-authorized at-home test. The Court can provide tests.

Judge Kaplan: Give my chambers your phone numbers and emails. But I think we can proceed this morning, and see how far we get. [People look confused. Spacey, at defense table, puts mask on.]

Now, despite what was said about Spacey's lawyer Keller testing positive for COVID, testimony of Rapp's expert Rocchio continues (!)

Rocchio: Attempted sexual interactions can impact -- Judge Kaplan: Members of the jury, I will instruct you as to the law.

Rocchio: I took a trauma inventory... Spacey's (second) lawyer: Objection, this invades the province of the jury, it goes to causation. Motion in limine number three. Judge Kaplan: Overruled.

On cross examination of Rapp's expert Rocchio by Kevin Spacey's lawyer: Q: Attorneys refer patients to you, right? Rocchio: Yes. Judge Kaplan: Do you consider what you did for Mr. Rapp in this case treatment? Rocchio: No.

Judge Kaplan: Folks, I have to take a break. [People wander around; some speculate if the call has to do with the trial going forward, unlike the US v. Trevor Milton / Nikola trial, which paused 9 days after lawyer tested positive for COVID). Thread will continue.

Judge Kaplan returns, and this is what he says: Members of the jury, in the morning I may have seemed to express skepticism about what Dr Rocchio was saying. You are not to consider that.

Spacey's lawyer: Are you aware Mr. Rapp said his boyfriend hit him multiple times? Rapp's lawyer: Objection! Judge Kaplan: Sustained. Rocchio: I'm not sure --

Judge Kaplan: The objection was sustained. They're back, cross: Spacey's lawyer: Did you review deposition of Anthony's brother Adam? Rocchio: Yes Spacey's lawyer: Let's talk PTSD. Requirement C is persistent avoidance of stimulae -

- I'm reading this out of the book. Rocchio: That's the heading.

Spacey's lawyer: Avoiding reminders that arouse traumatic memories... Mr. Rapp told you he avoids like that, right? Spacey's lawyer: But Mr. Rapp went to see Lost in Yonkers with Kevin Spacey in it. He didn't have an electric shock when he saw it, right?

Rocchio: No. Spacey's lawyer: And Mr. Rapp saw L.A. Confidential, right? Rocchio: Yes

Spacey's lawyer: You wrote that Mr. Rapp had "tears in his eyes" - did he? Rocchio: I wrote it. It happened a number of times. Spacey's lawyer: You are aware that he is an actor, right?

Spacey's lawyer: Dr Rocchio, you found that when he was 10 or 11, before 1986, Mr. Rapp engaged in oral sex, right? Rocchio: Right. Spacey's lawyer: And Rapp beat up a boyfriend who wanted to leave him?

Rocchio. Yes. He wrote about it.

The trial ended at 3:41 pm.

IX.

What was Team Spacey implying, eliciting that Anthony Rapp had oral sex at 11? That he had wanted want Spacey did to him? That he had led Spacey on? Or that no other victims of Spacey should come forward, as they and their families would be raked through the coals by Keller, COVID or no COVID?

COVID did not stop the Kevin Spacey trial on Monday and a good thing it was, at least from the POV of Spacey and the media. He took the stand and right out of the gate said, "My father was a white supremacist and neo-Nazi." People in the courtroom did double takes, even more so when Spacey turned on the water works. How could Rapp compete with this?

Things they got nitty gritty, with Spacey saying he found that it was a studio apartment he had lived in, not a one-bedroom. The apology to Rapp? It was written by his spokespeople, he had not believed in it and added the word "if" at each point.

IX. In the Courtroom

Before jury comes in, the scheduling: Spacey testimony will be today. Plaintiff (Rapp) has just rested his case. Spacey moves under Rule 50a for a judgment as a matter of law, will file memo "over the lunch hour."

Judge Kaplan: Over the lunch hour?

Spacey's lawyer: There was only incidental contact with the plaintiff's buttocks, even as told. It is plaintiff's burden to show that the claim-revival applies.

Judge Kaplan: I'm not going to grant that, at least now. The jury could infer it was for gratification

Rapp's lawyer: You are a 14-year-old boy wriggling out from under a 26-year-old man, who asks if he wants to stay. There was a battery and then this man [Spacey] pursued him

[Spacey's lawyer is quoting Judge Kaplan's ruling in Giuffre v. Prince Andrew back to him. But in this case, defense motion(s) not granted]

Judge Kaplan: I'm not going to grant that now. OK, bring the jury in. I'm going to tell them they'll get the case this week.

Judge Kaplan: We'll have the Barrowman deposition played, and then the defense's first witness, Mr. Spacey. Deposition (with Jennifer Keller) starts playing, stops. Judge Kaplan: Oh no.

[Barrowman was represented at the deposition by David Wright Tremaine LLP.] Barrowman: For the previous deposition I was in my flat in Cardiff, Wales where I film a show for iTV. It took 30 to 40 minutes. Q: When did you last speak to Mr. Rapp? Barrowman: 1998

Barrowman: I played Cole Porter's lover in a biopic. My sister and I have written a series of Y/A novels. There's also my first autobiography. Q: It's non-fiction, right. Barrowman: Yes, non-fiction.

Barrowman: I met Mr Rapp when he came to our school for the play Oliver. We would go out to Pop n' Fresh Pie.

Q: Did you see Mr. Rapp in NY? Barrowman: Yes. I stayed with him & his mother, & we went to see a play, after which we were in Jack Lemmon's dressing room

 Barrowman: Then we went to the Limelight. I had vodka and tonic from a plastic cup.

Q: In your book you say you drank vodka with Drew Barrymore.

Barrowman: I was told she was in the club.

Q: Did you see her?

Barrowman: No. So what I wrote was an interpretation.

Q: Did Mr. Spacey touch you at the Limelight?

Barrowman: Maybe on the dance floor we did something silly like dance the Bump. Then we went to see his place. It was a studio flat - sorry, I mean apartment. There was a bed.

Barrowman: You could see Jersey out the window. Anthony went to the bathroom and Kevin Spacey put his arm on me. I already knew I was gay. I was flattered that an older man was showing an interest in me.

Q: You were 19. Barrowman: Yes.

Barrowman: Afterward I sent Mr. Spacey flowers. He somehow called my mother... Later I saw Anthony in London, he was doing "Rent." We had dinner and I told him what had happened with Kevin Spacey. And he said something happened a following weekend, he got laid on

 OK, after a break, Defense: We call Kevin Spacey. Scolnick: Are Mr. Rapp's allegations true? Spacey: They aren't.

Scolnick: Mr. Rapp has criticized you for being private about your sexual orientation. Have you been private about other things? Spacey: Yes. My family.

Spacey: "My father was a white supremacist and a neo-Nazi." Then my hatred of bigotry began. I was embarrassed to bring anyone home. My best friend in high school was Jewish. I couldn't bring him home.

Spacey: My mother loved movies and music. I liked to make her laugh. Then my father sent me to military school. I got kicked out for having too many fights. The school liked fights.

Judge Kaplan: Hold on

 Spacey: My father would ask if I was gay, since I liked theater. He would use a hurtful word that begins with F. I had relationships with women as well. But so has Mr. Rapp. It's my choice. We have to respect that it is a difficult process.

Q: Did you do what Mr. Holtzman said you did?

Spacey: No.

Q: Mr. Holtzman says he recognized you from a program at the Public Theater. Were you on it?

Spacey: No I was not.

Spacey: I was really determined I did not want to wait on tables. Rapp's lawyer: Objection!

Judge Kaplan: He's asking how he got a job at the Public Theater. Overruled.

Spacey: I got past Dolores and Mr. Rapp said, Come on in. I told him my sob story. I was hired

Spacey: I had to get the car washed. I had to deliver the dry cleaning to his apartment on 10th Street.

Q: Did you type letters for him?

Spacey: I did.

Q: Let me show you a letter--

Rapp's lawyer: Objection! Judge: Come to the sidebar. [Whispering]

Q: Tell me about the Save the Theaters campaign.

Spacey: Mr. Papp worked to save two theaters - the Morosco and the Helen Hayes - from demolition for a hotel. The Honorable Thurgood Marshall issued a stay.

Q: Were you photographed? Spacey: Yes.

Spacey: Later I became the pinch hitter for most parts in Hurly Burly. I was getting sued for not paying rent, all over Manhattan. Then I got the role in Long Day's Journey into Night. Then I got the apartment - the best thing about it was the view

IX (con't) In the Courtroom

OK - after (long) lunch break, they're back.

Judge Kaplan: Mr. Spacey, or Mr. Fowler, tell me how you'd referred to be referred to.

Spacey: Spacey is fine.

Easel is pulled out, to demonstrate apartment lay-out.

Q: What about your personal life in 1986? Did you drink?

Spacey: Socially. But Long Day's Journey into Night was very demanding.

 Q: Did you use any drugs in 1986 in New York? Spacey: Not in New York. Q: Did you throw parties?

Spacey: Only 1. And not in May.

Q: What would happen after the performances?

Spacey: I'd often end up in Mr. Lemmon's dressing room. He'd say, "Wasn't I wonderful tonight?" [Spacey says it in a Jack Lemmon voice] Then I'd take a taxi to 66th Street and 2nd Avenue.

Spacey: In late 1987, I got a TV show, and I saw myself with a cigarette and a beer and it was 9:30 am. I said to myself, if I keep this up I'll be a barstool saying, It could have been me. So I stopped for eight years.

Spacey: When I met then in Jack Lemmon's dressing room, Anthony Rapp seemed like a boy, and John Barrowman appeared to be man.

Spacey's lawyer: Let me know you a photo.

Rapp's lawyer: Voir dire? [Then] No objection.

Q: Where did you all go to dinner?

Spacey: There are many restaurants, Joe Allen's and others. I don't remember which one we went to. I was focused on Mr. Barrowman. We had a drink at the Limelight. I danced with him.

Spacey: I said, Do you want to meet my dog? And we took a cab up to 66th Street. John and I saw on the bed, there was something going on. It has been testified that Mr. Rapp went to the bathroom. When he came out and we went downstairs. I had to walk my dog.

Spacey: Now later there was the Me Too movement. I think it had an impact because the claims against Harvey Weinstein were investigated for a year.

Spacey's lawyer: Did you get this email from Mr. Vary?

Spacey: Yes, the *journalist* [like in air quotes]

Spacey: Then the article came out. My publicists said, You have to apologize, you can't push back, they're going to call you a victim-blamer.

 Q: Did you team tell you that you had to express respect for Mr. Rapp, and regret?

Spacey: Yes. But I insisted that we use the word "if." Take it seriously but not factually.

 Q: Were you told to go out and do an interview about your sexuality, a bigger story?

Spacey: Yes. I was ready to put my sexuality behind myself. Lawyer: Let's take a break.

They've back. Spacey: Since the plane that I was on, on an AIDS mission, was owned by Jeffrey

Epstein, it was being reported I had gone to Pedo Island. Yes, I met Jeffrey Epstein. But I never went to any island.

Spacey: It was also being reported that in a pizzeria basement in DC, along with Anderson Cooper and Hillary Clinton, I was eating babies.

Spacey's lawyer: And that's false, right?

Spacey: Yes, it's false.... I was accused by the gay community of trying to change the subject (sniffles or sobs)

Rapp's lawyer: Objection. Judge: Overruled.

Spacey: I see why people thought that. That's mine, I have to own it. And I deeply sorry. (Leans forward, sobbing)

Note: This is not about a DC pizzeria basement - Epstein's Africa junket with Bill Clinton et al was a long trip. More later - they're back.

 Spacey: There were even people saying I should issue my statement before the article came out. But I thought I might learn from the article. Spacey's lawyer: Is this an email you wrote to Evan Lowenstein? Spacey: Yes

Spacey's lawyer: In it you say you had a dream that made you realize, what?

Spacey: That I didn't have a bedroom until 1991. I had a dream about Jack Lemmon, he visited me at 302 West 12th, and wrote me a letter to the board as Waverly Place.

Now Rapp's lawyers say they want to argue to expand the scope of cross examination of Spacey. So jury has been excused.

Rapp's lawyer: There is an inference that Mr. Spacey is sexual attracted to boys. On direct he has said he is not interested in boys. And see Exhibit VV

Rapp's lawyer: The defendant has opened the door. So we have impeachment testimony. Justin Dawes was 16. I would like to confront Mr. Spacey with his testimony.

Judge Kaplan: Rule 608e -- Mr. Scolnick, control yourself.

Scolnick: Mr. Dawes was combative and disrespectful of counsel. We have Mr. Brown -- Judge: Remind me what he says. Scolnick: He contradicts Dawes. It's all a distraction.

Rapp's lawyer: Mr. Spacey is under indictment in the UK for this conduct, while in the Old Vic --

Judge Kaplan: Do you have witnesses? He has denied the complaint in the UK. The presumption of innocence applies in the UK too. We're not trying the English case

Judge Kaplan: So I'll await more filings.

X.

The mystery arose: Where was Doctor Elizabeth Loftus? She had testified in the Ghislaine Maxwell trial, and Spacey had paid her to testify in his. But then, they said they wouldn't call her. Rapp's team asked for a "missing witness" instruction. Clearly, Spacey didn't like what his expert Loftus had found. But what was it?

X. In the Courtroom

On October 18, after cross of Spacey, his expert Dr. Bardey - instead of the expert he first paid, Dr. Loftus of Ghislaine Maxwell trial fame, who apparently didn't say what Spacey wanted and so wasn't called as a witness.

OK - in Rapp v Kevin Spacey, cross examination of Spacey.

Rapp's lawyer: You wrote, If he maintains there was a bedroom, he'll have a problem, right?

Spacey: Yes. Rapp's lawyer: You wrote, if it was in my apartment downtown, he'd be 19, - but this meant, it might have happened, right?

Spacey: Not sexually, sir.

Rapp's lawyer: Has it been an important part of your life to combat bigotry? Spacey: Yes. Rapp's lawyer: Do you have WhatsApp? Spacey: Yes. Rapp's lawyer: You used WhatsApp to text Mr. Lowenstein, right? Spacey: I might have.

Rapp's lawyer: You wrote, maybe just maybe Anthony Rapp is down on his luck-- Spacey's lawyer: Objection. Not in evidence.

Judge: Sustained. Rapp's lawyer: I offer it in evidence. Spacey's lawyer: Objection, 403. Judge: Sustained. Rapp's lawyer: Nothing further

Spacey's lawyer: Next witness is Dr. Alexander

Bardey. You are a forensic psychiatrist? Bardey: Yes. I went to SUNY Stony Brook School of Medicine then NYU, on staff at Bellevue. I head forensic psychiatry for Nassau County. I deal with malingering a lot

Spacey's lawyer: Mr. Rapp's expert Dr. Rocchio diagnosed Mr. Rapp with PTSD. Do you agree? Dr. Bardey: I do not. I met with him for about two & a half hour. Spacey's lawyer: Why only 2 & 1/2? Dr. Bardey: I had his deposition. So I interviewed his husband & others

 Dr. Bardey: My take-away from Rocchio's testing was that it was inconsistent. Rapp's lawyer: Objection. This is not in the report.

Judge (after a time) This is 49 single spaced pages. Let's give the jury a break as I read it. Break taken - thread will continue We're back. Spacey's lawyer: Any more sexually traumatic incidents for Mr. Rapp? Bardey: He was seduced by a 40-year-old actress when he was 16 or 17.

Spacey's lawyer: That could be traumatic? Rapp's lawyer: Objection. Judge: Sustained. Spacey's lawyer: Are you aware that Mr. Rapp engaged in sex with boys while 11 and 12? Dr Bardey: Yes. So I found no change in behavior after the alleged incident in 1986.

Dr. Bardey: I found he has aspects of narcissistic personality disorder. Spacey's lawyer: Would a person like that, if they lost a beauty contest or an election, claim they hadn't lost? [There is laugher, and an objection by Rapp's lawyer. Sustained.]

Judge says, Let's have a sidebar. Jurors, take a break. Spacey's lawyer: I'm staying on the right side of wrong. I'm not asking if he thinks Mr. Rapp is lying. Rapp's lawyer: They are trying to back into it. Judge: We have a contemporaneous objection rule.

Spacey's lawyer: Judge, if could just -- Judge Kaplan: My late great senior partner, who sat on this court, had a saying, When the judge is ruling in your favor, get out of the courtroom well... before he changes his mind. Jury is called back in.

But not for long - after an objection about a question to Dr Bardey on cross, Judge Kaplan says he'd like to review something, so sends jurors home. Now with jurors out of the courtroom, a last burst of argument about Dr. Loftus (also in Maxwell trial)

 Spacey put Dr Loftus on his witness list - but now, he's not calling her. Can jury to be told that? That is, is Rapp entitled to a missing witness charge? Judge: Where does she reside?

A: California.

Judge: I'll think about it overnight.

XI.

The final day of evidence was full of fights around Spacey's expert Doctor Bardey. He'd called Rapp a narcissist, or on cross examination, exhibit aspects of narcissistic personality disorder. Apparently, anyone who did not like being ignored could qualify for this. Kurt Wheelock wondered if his ongoing response to the United Nations throwing him out and banning his would qualify for this. Daily he emailed in questions, then shot video of the UN noon briefing, voicing over his outrage, only sometimes funny. There was the UN correspondent who had done a fundraiser with Ghislaine Maxwell, the same Maxwell whom

Kevin Spacey had posed with on the dual thrones in the UK....

XI. In the Courtroom

OK - Rapp v. Kevin Spacey trial now in last day of evidence, cross of Spacey's Dr. Bardey. Rapp's lawyer: So there were tests that Dr. Rocchio performed, that found Anthony Rapp was reporting his symptoms accurately, right?

Dr. Bardey: Correct. Rapp's lawyer: So they found him to be an honest reporter -- Judge: I used on this. Don't use the phrase. Rapp's lawyer: What did Dr Rocchio score Mr. Rapp, out of 63?

Dr Bardey: I don't remember. Rapp's lawyer: Page 11. You don't have Dr Roccio's report with you? Dr Bardey: I do not. Rapp's lawyer: So I show it to you. 19 out of 63. But you called it off the charts

Rapp's lawyer: How much do you charge Mr. Spacey in this case? Dr Bardey: $500 an hour. Rapp's lawyer: So you've gotten $45,000. You're a paid expert, right? Dr. Bardey: My time is compensated appropriately.

Rapp's lawyer: You spoke to Mr. Rapp's friend Detective Snow -- Spacey's lawyer: Objection! This has been ruled on! Judge Kaplan: Sustained. Rapp's lawyer: Did Mr. Snow say Mr. Rapp was one of the best people he knew -- Spacey's lawyer: Objection! Judge: Sustained

Re-direct. Spacey's lawyer: Did you read that Ken would get upset at Mr. Rapp of staying in touch with people from his distant past? Did Ken try to stop it? Spacey's expert

Bardey: Yes. Ken said he felt threatened. Break is taken. We're back. Spacey's lawyer: Mr. Rapp was asked if he had experience fear and shame, right? Dr Bardey: He said yes - and 75% of the time. Spacey's lawyer: This is what you mean by off the charts, yes? Dr. Bardey: Correct. I

Spacey's lawyer: You know Zoom, all of us do unfortunately - Mr. Rapp could have turned off Gallery View and not seen Mr. Spacey in the depositions and proceedings, right? Spacey's expert Bardey: Yes.

Spacey's lawyer: If Mr. Rapp, of all the in-person proceedings, only came to the one with a lot of press where Mr. Spacey was going to testify, would that be consistent with PTSD? Spacey's expert Bardey: No.

Re-cross (we're getting to the end) Rapp's lawyer: So you were not interested to know how he felt being deposed in this case? Spacey's lawyer: Objection, argumentative. Rapp's lawyer: Let me rephrase. Might it have been helpful to ask?

Bardey: It wasn't a factor

 Rapp's lawyer: Did you ask Mr. Rapp if he knows how to cut Mr. Spacey's face out of Zoom? Spacey's expert Bardey: No.

After rounds of re-re-direct and re-re-cross, "the Defense rests." Judge Kaplan told jurors to return tomorrow for closing arguments.

And they did...

XII.

Kurt Wheelock was going back to listen to Randy Fowler. A podcaster had asked him about Epstein;

he's answered about his brother on the thrones with Epstein's "female accomplice." Was Randy too a narcissist, for not liking being cut off by his brother after being sexually assaulted by their father?

Judge Kaplan had shaved Rapp's case down to its minimal claim: assault. He'd mused, before the charging conference, about whether as told Spacey had intended the pin-down to sexually gratify not only himself, but also 14-year-old Anthony Rapp. Rapp's lawyer said Spacey had meant to get consent -- not that a 14-year-old can legally consent, of course. Still, the closing arguments would happen. And Kurt Wheelock would be there.

XII: In the Courtroom, Last Day

OK - now Rapp v. Kevin Spacey closings arguments, with Rapp's lawyer going first.

Rapp's lawyer: We heard of [Spacey's lawyer] Ms. Keller that facts are stubborn things. And they are. So let's consider them. There is no evidence that Anthony was envious of John Barrowman, and Mr. Spacey's sexual interest in him.

Rapp's lawyer: Nothing in this record shows that Mr. Rapp at 14 had sexual feelings for Mr. Barrowman. They used this in their opening because they needed to prove it to win. And they didn't prove it. We'll talk about that night. But Ms. Keller overstated

Rapp's lawyer: We heard from Andrew Holtzman, that Spacey came into his office with a noticeable erection and attacked me. That's what happened that day. Do you think if there was dirt on Holtzman they wouldn't have brought it out?

Rapp's lawyer: Let's talk about 1986 and the night that brings us here. Kevin Spacey laughed and cried and did a Jack Lemmon interpretation. But there's an awful lot of things that Kevin Spacey does not remember. What did he say after Anthony Rapp came forward?

Rapp's lawyer: Mr. Spacey in his own email said he was heavily involved in drugs and alcohol. He said, I was drinking heavily and doing drugs. But now he says, the play was so demanding he didn't do either.

Rapp's lawyer: Outside the presence of this lawsuit, he admits to drugs and alcohol. Now he sees it doesn't look good and changes it. It lacks credibility. It's no honest. It taints everything.

Rapp's lawyer: Even months after Mr. Rapp came forward, Mr. Spacey is writing to his buddy that he doesn't remember. Either he's lying to his friend, or he truly has no memory. But they he claims it all came back to him when he saw the article. It's not honest.

Rapp's lawyer: They go and depose John Barrowman. He too says Spacey took them out to dinner then to the Limelight. It was a forerunner to Studio 54, a disco in a church with lights and music and Page Six. He takes a 14-year-old to a hot club.

Rapp's lawyer: How is it appropriate to make a pass at a 19-year-old when a 14-year-old is in the bathroom? That's their defense. And why can Anthony sketch the apartment so well? Even if there's no door, does it mean he is lying? Is that what comes up for you?

 Rapp's lawyer: And after Spacey picks him up like a groom docs and bride and Anthony escapes to the bathroom, when he comes out Spacey doesn't say he's joking, he asks, Don't you want to stay? This was trauma. But they say he just wants to bring Spacey down.

Rapp's lawyer: If this were only about bringing Mr. Spacey down, couldn't he have come up with a better story? More with the hands? They said Dr Rocchio is a paid expert. She testified two days without notes. Dr Bardey charges more, $500 an hour versus $450

 Rapp's lawyer: If you call a man a liar, you've got to give him a motive. Professional jealousy, at a time that Anthony is at the height of his career. Now it's homosexual rage. But Anthony said coming out was everyone's decision.

Rapp's lawyer: It doesn't matter where the story was published. Anthony came forward out of guilt, frankly, that he hadn't come forward before. He didn't tell his mother until the day she died.

Rapp's lawyer: Anthony has done this to hold Kevin Spacey accountable. Now they're saying that a person who was abuse has to avoid seeing the abuser, even on TV, or they're negligent.

Spacey's lawyer Jennifer Keller: Objection! We never argued that. Rapp's lawyer: I'll have a chance to speak to you again, after Ms. Keller and her excellent oratory skills. This happened. He has shared it with you. Thank you. Judge Kaplan: We'll take a break. You will be given menus.

 Now before she starts her closing argument, Jennifer Keller is hunched over with Spacey, planning what to say, how to respond to Rapp's closing? Drum roll.

Not hot mic moment for savvy Spacey: he pushes the defense table microphone to the side, and whispers in Keller's ear, like a baseball manager to a pitcher.

 Jury entering! Spacey's lawyer Jennifer Keller: I want to thank you jurors, on behalf of Mr. Spacey, for paying such close attention. I never talked about homosexual rage, never said Anthony Rapp was in love with Mr. Barrowman. I called him the Big Cheese in Joliet.

Keller: We are here because Mr. Rapp has falsely accused Mr. Spacey, of an incident that never occurred, in a room that does not exist. I am not going to call him Anthony. He is 51 years old. He is not a child.

Keller: Mr. Rapp tried to hitch his wagon to the

#MeToo movement - which was necessary, women were not believed. But Mr. Rapp's story is dependent on their being a wall, and a bedroom. And neither existed. And his story, it seems it comes from Precious Sons

 Keller: This was a party story that Mr. Rapp kept telling. But he can't ID a single witness from the party, can't describe them. There was no party. Mr. Rapp's book is in evidence, as Exhibit Triple B. He wrote he was annoyed at his mother following him.

Keller: The book is a confessional. It says it is about Rent but it is not. It is about babyhood, and his boyfriend trying to leave him - except, the Kevin Spacey story is not there. And it's from 2006. It is not the work of a private person, let's put it that way

 Keller: Yes, I asked Mr. Rapp is, being on Star Trek, he moved from the bathroom to the room via a Transporter. Yes we deposed Mr. Rapp first. Because, on the studio, we needed to lock him down so he couldn't, pardon me, wriggle out

Keller: This turns out to be one of the shortest parties in history. Was it a half hour party? This only make sense is no one is every going to ask you about the details. The devil is in the details. This party never happened.

 Keller: Who does he tell about it? He tells his brother. [Note: Kevin Spacey's brother Randy Fowler may be been nearly entirely absent from this trial, but going forward will not be?]

Later, he tries to get The Advocate to publish a story in 2001 after Mr. Spacey gets an Oscar for American Beauty. It's strange - if Mr. Rapp was a gay activist, you wouldn't think he'd want to out and claim a child molester

 Keller: Do you remember Brian Williams? Highly respected news man who lied about being in a helicopter gunship that was hit. He was exposed. President Reagan told a story how as an army photographer saw the Nazi death camp - never happened, never left the US.

Keller: No one saying Anthony was in a homosexual rage which is, I might say, an offensive phrase. But Mr. Rapp got a lot of attention from it. He got an "Out and Equal" champion award - and told a false story, about being inspired by the #MeToo NYT op-ed

 Keller: Imagine it were 2052 and someone accused you- Rapp's lawyer: I have to object. Judge: Sustained. Keller: A person is accused. How do you defend yourself? A bad person says, This person is a liar. But this is Me Too time. Mr. Spacey is told he must apologize

Keller: Mr. Spacey gives Mr. Rapp the benefit of the doubt and issues a non-apology apology. He insists on "if." And in Feb 2018 Mr. Spacey writes, It's like hearing about a person I do not know. He muses it might have been later, when he was 19

Keller: If I've offended people, the way I cross examined Mr. Rapp, I'm sorry. But it's a necessary part of getting to the truth. It's fair to say that Precious Sons was the big moment in Mr. Rapp's life. It got some reviews but no one went to see it.

 Keller: If it's bad judgment by a 26-year-old to take a 19-year-old and a 14-year-old to the Limelight. I'm 69 but even I know clubs are not jumping at 7:30 pm. That's the time to take kids to a club. Is it evil? I like it was nice, actually.

Keller: Mr. Spacey because a global star. Mr. Rapp? Stardom did not follow him. It's hard to make a living as a working actor. Him saying there's no envy is like me saying I don't even Ruth Bader Ginsburg. It's not credible

 Keller: You can Google him anywhere in the world -- Judge Kaplan: No you can't. There's no evidence in this trial about Google. Go on. Keller: Mr. Rapp is well known now for taking down one of the greatest actors of his generation.

Keller: Dr Rocchio didn't talk about the baseline. So, Dr Bardey, of course we had to retain someone. He didn't go to Maine. We went down the street, to a NYU professor, who works at Bellevue. He can't say, but I'm going to say, that Mr. Rapp was faking it. Keller: Dr Bardey says he show narcissism. What is that?

[From the creative commons: 'Narcissism' comes from Ovid's Metamorphoses...When Narcissus rejects the nymph Echo the gods punish him, making him fall in love with his own reflection in a pool of water.

Keller: Our star witness is the floor plan of the

small studio apartment. Mr. Rapp has given an impossible story. So I urge you, reject any compromise verdict, awarding $1 of damages. It. Didn't. Happen. 1 penny is too much.

 Keller: The first question on the verdict form is, Did Mr. Rapp prove by a preponderance of the evidence - he did not. Vote no. Judge Kaplan: In ten minutes, the rebuttal and my charge. [And then? This thread will continue]

 We're back, with Rapp's rebuttal and then jury charge. Rapp's lawyer: The proof has to come in the case, not in argument. Mr. Barrowman never told Anthony about what he said Mr. Spacey did, until the late 90s... Let's put up the verdict sheet. Judge Kaplan: No.

Rapp's lawyer: The first question on the verdict form is, Did we prove by a preponderance of the evidence that Mr. Spacey touched -- Judge Kaplan: If you can't restrain yourself, you'll have to sit down. Rapp's lawyer: We have proved it by a preponderance.

 Rapp's lawyer: Why are you getting on top of a child on a bed? There's a question, Did he do it to gratify Mr. Rapp's sexual desire? Keller: Objection! Beyond the scope! Judge: I'll allow it.

Rapp's lawyer: Your award for the past should reflect all the ways it has impacted Anthony in the past. And as to the future, Dr. Rocchio says it continues. Don't let him get it away this time.

Judge Kaplan: Counsel's personal wishes are not to be considered.

Judge Kaplan: My instructions are going to be in 4 parts. It's going to be the shortest jury charge I've given in 28 years. 38 minutes later, instructions winding up.

Judge Kaplan: The exhibit will be sent in. Ladies and gentlemen, you may retire to deliberate. Keller says she is disappointed that Rapp's lawyer said, "I hope you don't let him away with it this time," which clearly implies there are other times. This was premeditated. There should be some kind of sanction.

Judge Kaplan: I'm not going to do anything now.

Judge Kaplan: If there is a defense verdict, it's a

matter of professional conduct, if anything. If there's a plaintiff's verdict, it could be a matter for motion practice. Just like Mr. Rapp's answer about why did you bring this case. That's where we are.

OK - it's 4:02 pm and the plaintiff's team has reassembled at their table in the courtroom. The jury has reached a verdict - and it's hard to imagine it's for Rapp, if it's this fast.

Note: if the jurors answered Yes to Question 1, they'd have to go to Question 6. If they answered Yes to Question 2, they'd have to go to Questions 3, 4 & 5. But if two No's, they just send a note back: we have a verdict. Now Spacey at defense table. Drum roll.

Judge Kaplan: I'm advised that we have a verdict. Please bring in the jury.

Judge Kaplan: Clerk will publish the verdict. Question to jury. Answer: No.

Judge Kaplan: Is there a motion to dismiss the case?

Yes.

Dismissed.

It was over?

Or was it just beginning? American Ugly...

9 798359 313780